RAFAEL

DUEL IN

2

TIMES

VOL. 2

STEWART

> If you put your soul in every gesture of love, You will always feel like a flower ……

Note about rights

2 | Page

Reproduction of this book or parts of it in any form, nor that it be archived in a system or transmitted in any way or by any means — electronic, mechanical, photocopying, recording, or otherwise — is not authorized without prior written permission from the publishing house, except as provided by copyright laws in the United States of America. Unless otherwise indicated, the texts and opinions are those of the author.

Photographs By: Jonathan Xavier Gamboa / Quito, Ecuador

Content

Topic # 1 THE LOVING DUEL

Topic # 2 OVERCOMING THE LOSS OF YOUR JOB

Topic # 3 YOU CAN OVERCOME THE DEATH OF A CHILD

Topic # 4 THE LOSS OF A PET… CAN BE OVERCOME

Topic # 5 OVERCOME THE DEATH OF YOUR PARTNER

Topic # 6 FEELING OF SADNESS

Topic # 7 FEELING ANGRY

Topic # 8 FEELING OF GUILT

Topic # 9 FEELING OF ANXIETY

Topic # 10 EMOTIONAL FATIGUE

                    Rafael Stewart

RAFAEL
STEWART
RAFAEL STEWART
FOREVER, INC.
®™

Vol. 2

Here are different types of duels

Continuation of Vol. 1

Welcome to the no-judgment zone!

Topic 1

The Loving Duel

When a change is about to begin or you are on the path of change there may be obstacles, complexities, and setbacks, where do you stand? Let's discuss:

When you are going through the love affair, you should keep in mind that it is a process of emotional adjustment after a big breakup, during which various emotions and conditions compete. On this path you will go through different stages that can be explained individually, but they are not always presented in the same way or order. Emotions could overlap and mix with each other, but what you do have to keep in mind is that, to overcome this healing

process, you must experience pain and go through all

of them.

As in everything there are going to be good or

bad days, some better than others. On certain

occasions, what you thought was overcome or cured

could be felt again, and that is normal.

These are the various phases that you can go

through, better to say that if you are going to

experiment since it is part of the process of love grief.

1. Love and hate.

2. Heaviness and relief.

3. Loneliness and sociability.

4. Past and present.

5. Certainty and uncertainty.

In relation to the subject, you may notice that

emotions will dominate any attempt of your rational,

although as it will be possible to sit down to evaluate the benefits of your decision, if so, it is your decision. It is imperative that you do not fall into the betrayal of guilt or nostalgia for the love cycle that has closed. When you act to make the decision to separate or the other person decides to end, both will always be right, because it is what they want and think at that moment.

This could be valid points, for wanting or going through a love break:

1. Control over the other.

2. Jealousy.

3. Violence.

4. Questions to personal projects.

5. Intimate disagreements.

6. Disagreements with parenting.

7. And certain sexual difficulties

These can take a step in a relationship and bring it to an end.

It always begins in the stage of anger, wrath, quarrel, and not only with the other, but with oneself. And you will say things like Why did it happens to me? "Why couldn't I?" or perhaps "he did not know how to take care of myself or my needs." Then it is followed by great anguish for the new loneliness, the absence of the other, the knowledge that you will not be able to share more with that person, you could come to think that uncertainty for the future.

Here an instance stage will begin with a more real idea of what happened and what you must do to be better. This is where it is accepted that the decision [it does not matter who makes it] to separate had its true reasons and that you must continue with other projects, you will know that life does not end or stop due to a love failure.

As things happen, you must establish trust, personal security, appreciate and enjoy solitude, a crazy and immense desire to be with someone. Here things of being in a hurry to be with someone do not work (that one nail pulls another, it is a lie, one nail pushes another one deeper), however, you cannot be closed to believe in love. This will go through your mind while the break is fresh, but it is imperative to know that you must establish a great conviction that everything will happen and that you will overcome the past.

DEPENDENT PERSONALITIES:

There is nothing worse than depending on someone in a way that refuses to end a toxic relationship: not emotionally, much less physically. People like that tend to be slower and are tied to the idea that there is something left to follow. It is a total denial of not ending, and more of that is because of EMOCIAL LAZINESS, and deciding not to work with the breakdown of the relationship. This type of people lives thinking about their ex-partner, they are unable to focus their energies on other things, the obsession begins, they want to know everything about the other person, in real terms to continue in a relationship where the reproduction of the same problems is continued and themes.

Another way could be to look for ephemeral relationships that only bring a fleeting connection, that is nothing, maybe they listen to you and pure sex, keep in mind, it is a defensive way to mitigate the anger or contained violence of failure, creating more emotional instability. It is only done to go from couple to couple just to feel company. Obviously, the pain and fear will continue and will not leave the place where they are embodied in your being.

It is a mechanism to create a favorable fictional scenario, self-deception in a pleasant emotional state, when it is a way to reduce pain, pretending leads to NOTHING. In this type of relationship, it is seen more in men than women, since men are more emotionally illiterate and are not about expressing their feelings openly, [nor do we think that this is always the case], we must let our emotions flow and carry its course like a river reaching the sea.

If you continue this path you will begin to create something that is known as a damaged ego, which is a transitional emotion, just by knowing that gratification it is minor and in the end the pain will have to be dealt with once and for all. As this develops, it will be good for you to assume that you must continue living while the pain is encoded in your being. As it happens, you will begin to feel stronger, more confident, and with a greater capacity to understand the reasons. It will take its course and the sadness will end.

CHOOSE BY COMPARISON:

When you feel up to dating someone [partner form], you can fall into the trap of starting to compare potential people with whom you can date your past partner. Then the following is going to happen, you are going to choose the same thing you had, only in a physically different person, that is, to look for everything that the previous person made you feel, it is a very bad strategy, something that will lead you to NOTHING. In context, looking for someone like your ex-partner shows the mental constipation in which you live. You do not accept that it ended, and you hurt yourself and incidentally the other person [new partner] you will start a compulsive obsession that will lead to nothing. It may be that you also seek those types of relationships as well, out of fear of suffering. You must maintain connection with your emotions and your needs as an individual, do not look for a relationship when you know that you are wrong.

You just must focus on your needs to be able to build a better and more satisfying life and once that happens you will have a new relationship with yourself and in the process, you will find your new half.

The decision to break the relationship and those to bond with others should be independent processes. When you heal and complete the grieving process, you can find your new partner.

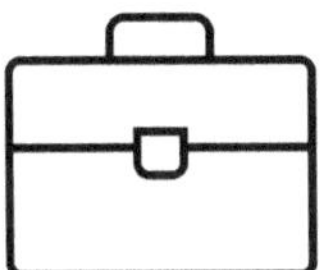

Topic 2

OVERCOME THE LOSS OF YOUR JOB

The person who is unemployed faces important changes in their life since you must adapt to the situation that is different from what you lived before and accepting the change is a bit difficult, but nothing that cannot be resolved. Everyone who has ever worked or works knows that a fear factor is losing your job through layoff, disability, or anything else. That instead is known as a DUEL, and I assure you that people who lose their job are affected economically, creating a large hole in finances and, incidentally, emotions, including self-esteem, may be affected.

It is difficult, but you must take immediate action to try to return to normality as before, since many things involve job loss. Even if you feel inferior, worthless or something, it is temporary and such thoughts are negative, and social pressure could aggravate those thoughts. All of this will influence the grieving process.

To overcome this process, I have created a short guide that you must implement for you to go through this duel quickly.

1. Avoid bad habits and personal inattention: do not live regretting things, lying on the bed or furniture. In difficult times, people become good friends with their beds or furniture, it is disastrous to live like this, or to fall into it. And that in part adds more negative and wrong thoughts. Being listless is a

very difficult and acute stage where you could find yourself because that is where personal carelessness begins, lack of hygiene, and perhaps you come to invent problems, or go through things that should not happen.

2. Do not be a prisoner of fear: when you go through these types of situations, a type of devaluation begins, and you will feel that the skills no longer exist and that you may also feel that the virtues disappeared. Being like this, it is obvious that you will feel that you will not be able to get out of that hole. However, you cannot allow despair to enter, or overwhelm your thoughts, you must find activities to be active. Doing sports, a new hobby, always you must keep your mind occupied so that it does not get bogged down in bad thoughts.

3. The goal is to look for work: you must establish a specific schedule and time to find another

job. It is something serious and something that you must fulfill since you will not be able to spend years searching for a job. With discipline and a real focus, you can find something fast. Also, you must have communication with family friends or colleagues because it is a way of knowing if there is something that they can offer you or know something. It's easy and it doesn't cost anything.

4. Organization and reduction of expenses: while this is happening, we must cut expenses that are unnecessary, things that do not have priority. You must know that it is important to do this to minimize the blow to the pocket. It is difficult but you cannot live in the same way as before since the salary that let you be as you were, was lost.

5. Training: don't be wasting time on things that will only set you back. Losing your job is not synonymous with doing things you didn't do before.

Keeping in mind that training does not mean anything bad, only that you can learn new skills and things that you may not know. Expand your knowledge and concepts so that you can be much more prepared for the next work adventure.

6. Do not lose enthusiasm and confidence: you must get away from all bad energy and vibes and very important negative feelings. Allow bad energies to overwhelm your mind, remember that it is easier to go through this duel if the mind is positive. To be able to have a new job, the key is to know that you are a professional and your value as a professional. In this way, it will be much easier to achieve the goal of a new job. You must have your own security, first.

You cannot feel defeated, you must learn not to lose CONFIDENCE in yourself. You well know that everything that happens, happens for the good, that is why being patient should be your immediate ally.

Don't feel bad about anything, everything will pass. A positive attitude will open doors for you.

Topic 3
YOU CAN OVERCOME THE DEATH OF A CHILD

Losing a child is a unique event and of extra-perplexed, it is one of the strongest pains that a mother and father can go through. In this type of loss, there is no comfort, there are no words that can be used to help get past the pain that is felt. But there is a process to overcome the loss and move on, keeping in mind that pain is the only way to overcome the pain.

I'm going to help you in a new way so that maybe if you go through this or you went through that or you are going through this, you will have an extra hand helping to improve your life.

The loss of a son

This event is extremely stressful and with the greatest emotional and personal impact that a person can suffer. Going through this type of loss, everything planned is paused, and one begins to live in a state of imbalance in life. All kinds of expectations that you may have had about life cease with the loss of a child. Likewise, very intense emotional reactions will also appear, such as sadness, guilt, anger and fear. I invite you to continue reading so that I can help you face this loss.

<u>Overcoming the death of a child</u>

You cannot overcome the death of a child if you do not fulfill your grief, which is a natural process and is necessary to understand how complex it can be. The stages and emotional reactions are unique and are experienced at different times. Overcoming a grief is a matter of accepting what happened, accepting the circumstances, and creating a new vision for the future to come.

<u>Stages:</u>

1. _ACCEPTANCE_: the most difficult part to face is acceptance, the reality of what you are experiencing. Accepting the death of a child is going to be very difficult and tends to provoke feelings about the loss, coming to feel that nothing is happening. It is imperative that parents become aware of the irreversibility of the event, achieving intellectual and emotional acceptance. In this process of acceptance, things like "why" will be very frequent and, incidentally, also look for hypotheses as to why what

happened, although thinking about that is far from reality. There is no answer to the questions that may come up or something convincing that helps the parents lessen the painful feelings, nothing will be to the satisfaction of the parents. Faced with this situation, it will be understood not to answer questions that cannot be understood or can be understood. Everything with measure.

2. _THE EMOTIONS AND PAIN_: to face the pain and the emotions that loss entails, it will be necessary to evaluate all the emotions that are taking shape in you. The intensity of the feelings can vary. _Let's discuss:_

a. Sadness: this emotion will be present for a long time; it will begin to always appear, and it will invade you in many moments. Avoiding sadness does not show that you are overcoming the loss, on the contrary, you should under no circumstances avoid sadness, not hide it, and even less ignore it. Keep in mind that if you force yourself to avoid it sooner or later it will return sharper. Being sad about the death of a child is essential and you always have to face it. Allow yourself to express what you feel, cry, vent, scream, the pain will not change, but it will make you feel better.

b. Guilt: thousands of questions will come to your mind, and that's when the famous emotion of guilt will begin to take shape in your life. And feel guilty, it is not that you did something wrong, it is just a mechanism of the mind to face the situation, perhaps wanting to change position with the lost son, said reality will not change, but it will confuse your mind. It is inevitable that since the realism of what is lived changes, as the days pass the guilt in a real way, it will come back to you, and it is a normal part of the duel, but in the form of reproach, it will be more directed to the have a good day you think you miss your son's memory. Being happy one day does not betray the memory of your child, feel good, and never reproach yourself.

c. Anger / rage: it is normal to feel anger or pissed, it is part of the pain that is happening, during the loss of a child. Anger occurs because you cannot go back in time, because you cannot change things and you have to keep in mind that it can be located in yourself or in others. It is not that your character changes or you are different or that you are bad, you have gone through a unique loss and then all kinds of emotions pass. Through these emotions you will be able to transmit the frustrations that you are experiencing now, whether you want to or not, you have to accept and channel anger and rage.

d. Anxiety: in the grieving process, anxiety will visit your mind, and it usually happens more at the beginning of the grief, when you cannot accept what happened. It tends to be seen a lot when the attachment figure is absent at the time. Anxiety has a habit of transforming pain.

e_Fear_: being afraid or feeling it is a normal emotion, the expectations of the future that you had were erased, and in your world thinking about a future is something unreal and uncertain. Fear must be overcome and viewed more as something temporary.

3. A NEW FUTURE: when you lose a child, you are going to consider the future and what you expected from life, in view of this, you must adapt to the new reality as soon as possible. When the reality of your child's death is accepted, you have already managed to understand, express, and stabilize emotions, you must enter the path of REORGANIZING YOUR LIFE and try to return to the new normal, achieving a balance between what you had and the future that is

ahead. You must readjust life in a new way, without forgetting the past, but with attention to what the future will be like.

How to overcome the death of an only child?

1. You must adapt to the future in any type of loss, because it will not matter if the loss has been of an only child or in a large family, the expectations of the future will always change in both cases. And in the same way the duel will take the course. The lost child can be emotionally relocated, managing to live without the child. Even if the duel is overcome and passes, feelings in other degrees will return, and before any type of relapse you must go back to work to save your emotions.

How to overcome the loss of a child in the womb?

2. The loss of a child in the womb will have the same type of process and the same pain as the loss of an

older one. Many think that since the son was not born, and even less did you see that the pain is different, and that is a wrong thought. They need to know that the emotional bond begins a few weeks into the pregnancy. This connection sets up thousands of expectations of how they are going to do things, what you had prepared, and everything related to the child. It is when all life revolves around the baby. In the same way they must go through the duel since the baby occupies an important place in the lives of the parents.

How to overcome the death of a newborn child?

3. Losing a newborn child carries the same weight as any other form of loss, in the same way the bond created is still there, and even more so when it comes time to meet the child. The emptiness is serious since you leave the hospital or wherever without your child, empty-handed. Everything evaporates into the air,

nothing remains, just a bad memory and a total emptiness. Feelings of helplessness will come, and you will feel the same as any other type of loss. No one has the right to minimize the pain or the process just because they don't understand.

You must recognize and deal with pain. You must feel it and express it.

Topic 4

THE LOSS OF A PET ... CAN BE EXCEEDED

Pets are an essential part of many people's lives, likewise many are surprised by the emotions they feel after the death of the pet. You can feel guilty for the immense grief you feel. Keep in mind that pets are part of the family, our routines, and the home. Pets are known to be loved, and we also know that they are true friends and faithful.

Perhaps, you do not think that it is necessary to go through a duel, since it is a pet. But to overcome the death of a pet it is necessary to go through a duel, especially when it is truly loved and was part of the house. There are ties that were created with the pet and it is difficult for many to continue a normal life. Pets are more than property; they are part of oneself.

This type of grief usually happens more to the minors of the house and those people who only live with their faithful friend in life. These people should never be left alone, and it is imperative that you be attentive to the emotional state of each of the people, or your own if that is the case. There should be no shame in saying or feeling pain over the death of our pet. You know that you were all in tis life or part of it with your pet, and it is normal to feel listless in the face of death.

As in all the world, there will be people who will not understand this type of feelings or can value the sadness it causes (more common it tends to happen with people who see pets as property). Surrounding

yourself with people who love animals would be great

to make you feel comfortable and with people who do

understand the process and what it feels like.

THE PHASES OF THE DUEL:

If you lost a pet, you would understand these

points. It is necessary to talk about your pet and how

you feel about the absence. Those days are going to

be hard, but you must face the loss in your own way.

They will be bitter days but going through this is

essential to be well. Grief is nothing more than doing

an emotional adjustment process, where many

emotions will compete. Like all duels there will be

good days and others not so good, and sometimes

you may feel that you did not overcome anything.

5 points that make up part of the duel:

1. THE DENIAL: this is stage number 1; it occurs when the reality of the loss is denied. I mean, you won't believe the event happened. You cannot believe that it will not return or be present anymore.

2. THE ANGER: the anger will come to you, and perhaps against those who are close to you. It is the anger, rage, and fury that you feel when you know that, if it happened, that, if it is true, that it is no longer present, the impotence of not knowing what to do.

3. THE NEGOTIATION: it is a very interesting stage, it is when you try to make a deal, pact, or agreement. You think about the past, to analyze the lived situation and perhaps think that it would have been different or how the circumstances would have been differently. This is when all kinds of questioning occur.

4. DEPRESSION: here you experience anguish, fears, afflictions, and you can end up crying incessantly. You will feel guilt or regrets. It is accepted that death is irrevocable, and that we must continue living, without the physical presence of the pet that we lost.

5. ACCEPTANCE: here is also part of the preparation to be well, and to know that what happened. The certainty is already in conscience that, if it left, and it is necessary to return to life again. Be clear that it is not that you forget the loss but that you have to know that it is no longer there, and you have to move on.

A. You must learn to overcome sadness

B. Feel free to cry

C. Never blame yourself for what happened

D. Let good memories win over pain

DO NOT LOSE SIGHT OF THE FOLLOWING:

1. The impact that causes the death of your pet.

2. Give yourself a chance to be sad.

3. Feeling guilt is normal, and you should assimilate it as part of the process.

4. You must make an ally of patience.

5. Be aware that the pain may be intense and long-lasting.

There is no
established period
for the infliction to
be remitted, but
what is certain is
that it will.

Topic # 5

OVERCOME THE DEATH OF YOUR PARTNER

I think we have all had a partner, be it boyfriend or girlfriend. The more time they spend together, the stronger a breakup would be since it is out of habit or true love. In topic # 1 I talked about the breakup in the form of love grief, now I'm going to talk about a breakup that affects much more than a love breakup, and it is about the death of that person you chose to be together.

The passing of someone close to you is the worst feeling a person can go through. Nobody in this life is prepared to face the traumatic situation and nobody has the advice to help the pain pass quickly.

The feeling that nobody wants to experience and that

always grabs you in an unexpected way. Even if you

go through thousands of problems, death is

something transcendental and something that no one

wants for their partner, although that is how you may

think in times of anger. In this topic I focus on the

couple, but it should be noted that no matter what

kind of loss it is, the feeling will be the same.

One of the worst losses is the loss of your

partner. Of course, when you talk about your life

partner, the pain is serious. Just knowing that we lose

that person we love is a feeling of sadness. Everyone

is different but rest assured that no one has the

correct tools to process this, and everyone processes

death in different ways.

<u>I hope these tips are helpful to help you prepare</u>

<u>or grieve:</u>

1. **What can I do to overcome the death of my partner?**

A. ACCEPT THE DUEL: we are already clear that this is the worst feeling that a person can go through, but for the healing power to begin, you must accept and recognize that your partner is no longer there, that is, live the reality that will no longer come or will be present.

B. LET FEELINGS FLOW: Under no circumstances can we allow ourselves to repress our feelings. The healthiest thing is that everything works out, no matter how difficult the situation. Rest assured that you will have someone to vent with and it will be an essential part of healing the wounds created by the departure.

C. LIFE GOES ON: you cannot think that thinking that you should continue your life is selfish. There is nothing better than finding a way to get on with your life. Do not think that I tell you, forget about the person, but that you understand that life is going to run its course with or without the person.

D. TAKE CARE OF YOURSELF: we recognize that it is a bad time in your life, and that is respected, now you have to continue with the family, not neglect them, you have to be aware of those who depend on you and yourself (see Topic # 4 in Volume #1).

E. SUPPORT THE FAMILY: Not only are you in pain, it is essential that you recognize that your family will also be in pain. I mean recognize that you must support others in the family as well.

F. TIME: unfortunately, this word is trite, and it bothers many, but the only way someone is going to heal and can move on is for TIME to take its course.

There is nothing more than that, time.

Discover how strong you are ……. Death is part of this journey called life ……. It's not a goodbye, it's a see you soon.

Topic # 6

FEELING OF SADNESS

In this emotional dueling, different emotions always come, we have talked about them in many chapters and through other books that I have published, but this time I want to focus on certain emotions and go a little deeper.

Sadness breaks into life, this changes to become something annoying and that we surely want to eliminate, but sadness is part that makes up a psychic balance in everyone.

Is having emotions necessary?

Suppose we are driving our car and suddenly a red light appears on the dashboard and that light indicates that the car is running out of gas. If you focus on the information given, you will see that you will immediately find where to fill the gas tank. Using this example, emotions, in the same way, are indicative signals that direct our behavior depending on the situations that are being experienced. Of course, that helps us to make decisions and to adapt to the harsh reality, be it positive or negative.

What is sadness?

Sadness is an emotion that activates a psychological process that allows us to overcome losses, disappointments, or failures. It is vital in the life of each one of us. This allows you to establish a distance with painful situations so that you can encourage them to internalize the pain generated by them. Similarly, feeling sad helps to empathize with the sadness of others, thus creating the famous "support network."

Sadness manifests itself in different ways:

1. <u>Physical level:</u> crying, psychomotor retardation, downcast face, lack of appetite, sleep problems and more.

2. <u>Mental level</u>: attention is focused on the situation being experienced, difficulty having a blank mind, high concentration problems, intrusive thoughts about what is being experienced.

3. <u>Behavior level:</u> totally a person who is not motivated. Not interested in anything that may be living now.

When you feel sad, denying yourself is inevitable, isolating yourself so that the sadness process begins is normal, this is when you will begin to have alternate thoughts about what happens or happened, this will help you fit into life again. Incidentally, this is followed by the production of readjusting or reorganizing the behavior that is transmitted when you are sad, it is part of an adaptation to be able to live the new reality.

In conclusion, being sad is a useful emotion even though it hurts and is strong, it is a path that will open new doors in your painful recovery process.

How do I deal with sadness?

First, you must recognize the emotion, and that it is present, being aware of the emotion will help you work better with it.

Accept that sadness is not something that makes you weak, do not think that you will be vulnerable by perhaps feeling sad. It is a normal process which only you will know how to guide you and move on to the other emotions.

Even though you are sad, you must know that you must act, you must educate yourself to be able to eliminate the situation that is generating sadness, for example, if you are sad about an argument, keep in mind that by talking to the person in this case you can sort out. Going through a grief is different since the sadness of loss is not the same, you must find comfort in others, recognize that you need help. I have always said that you must let out all your emotions without fear of anything. It is legal and vital that everything that is inside comes out. Many takes refuge in drugs, alcohol, sex, isolation and although we can say I understand it, this happens when the person does not have the correct support network,

outside there may be thousands of people who can

speak or have an opinion, but few are trained to work

with issues like this. Never feel bad for wanting to

receive help from where you believe and not where

you are forced.

How to heal

A. Taking care of your physical health is reflected in

your emotions: Amplifying simple and healthy habits,

such as drinking more water, eating healthier,

exercising, or trying to sleep more at night, can have

a positive effect on your mood.

B. Try to live your life: it is meaningful to remember

the things you used to do and what made you happy.

However, do not feel well, going for a walk, reading a

good book or watching your favorite movie can bring

you some joy. Allow yourself to be happy.

C. <u>Seek support from your family and friends:</u>

Although grieving is a personal process, seek

understanding and the company of someone close to

you, especially if you feel alone. Don't be afraid to

share your feelings and bond with others.

D. <u>Be patient with the process:</u> There is no schedule

for pain. For some people, the pain can last a long

time, mainly if it is due to the death of someone close.

In fact, you may never completely get over it: listening

to a song or remembering the anniversary of an event

can make your pain more intense, even if you thought

you were over it. But over time, the pain gets shorter.

It may take years for the pain of grief to completely fly

away.

E. <u>Go to therapy:</u> Sometimes pain can affect your

ability to live a healthy life and you may need added

support from a professional. Talk to your doctor or

find a therapist if:

1. *Your pain prevents you from doing normal daily activities, such as going to work, keeping your house in order, or taking care of yourself*

----

2. *You withdraw socially from the people in your life*

----

3. *You feel that life is not worth living*

----

4. *You think about hurting yourself*

Topic # 7

FEELING OF ANGER

How many have not been angry, annoyed, cursed, or send someone to hell? Answer this question in your mind and then read on. Anger is a totally normal emotion and even a healthy thing. But do not think that it is a walk-through Disney, when you lose control, it becomes destructive, it can cause thousands of problems at work, home, personal relationships and in general the quality of life. If you get to this point, the emotion controls you before you control it and from there it is difficult to get out.

What is anger?

First, it is an emotional state that varies in intensity. It ranges from something simple like irritation to intense fury and anger. Like all kinds of emotions, it carries with it psychological and biological changes. I tell you, when you get angry, your heart rate and blood pressure skyrocket, adding to this hormone like adrenaline and norepinephrine.

You may not even know why you are getting angry, but it could be caused by external or internal events, and in the case of a duel, it manifests itself in both. You have the green light to get angry with someone specific or because of something that happened, or it can also be out of concern or taciturn due to personal problems. And in a mourning the infallible anger for the loss of the person or event, and it is part that is lived, you cannot say I will not be angry because it is a lie.

Express anger

A natural and instinctive way to express is to respond aggressively. Anger is key to adapting to threats, and inspires intense feelings, easily aggressive, bringing with it behaviors you do not act to fight or change. In other words, to survive you need a certain degree of anger. Always keep in mind that you control the emotions, not the emotions to you.

However, you cannot attack people or objects that may irritate or annoy you, keep in mind that you are not the only one in the world and even if you are submerged in anger, you could have legal consequences, you have to know how to work and adjust when you pass by this stage. Each uses the way they think is correct, whether it is a conscious or unconscious process to deal with angry feelings. This is so:

EXPRESS, SUPPRESS AND CALM

I'm going to tell you something, you can be angry, feel bad but your right and correct way is to be angry with firmness without being AGGRESSIVE. Always be clear that you must learn how to let know what the needs are and how you want it to be done without hurting others who have no fault. Do not confuse being firm with being arrogant and much less demanding, it is respecting others and more importantly respecting yourself.

On the other hand, repressing anger and automatically converting or redirecting it. This happens when anger is content, you stop thinking about anger and your concentration turns to something positive. The goal here is to inhibit or suppress anger and to change your behavior in a more positive way. Being like this obviously will not let anger out. Be aware that being like this is going to affect your physical health, be careful with that.

Being with unexpressed anger will generate countless problems for you. Perhaps something that you had not heard, can lead you to lead pathological expressions of anger; Example, a passive-aggressive behavior (you take it out on the wrong people or things, for not having a motive) or a lasting cynical and hostile attitude. If after the duel you continue to criticize, complain, they are obvious patterns of people who do not know how to control their emotions, especially ANGER.

Being like this some people will not have success in their grief or normal life. One note, this applies to all types of anger, grieving or not.

Lastly, you must calm yourself inside. In other words, not only controlling your external behavior but also controlling your intimate responses.

Anger management

Managing anger is in part reducing feelings and awakening the physiological it provokes. If you cannot get rid of the things or people that make you angry, or much less avoid them, you will be able to control your reactions.

Are you very angry? <answer this question in your mind.

There are tests that measure the intensity of angry emotions, how prone to anger you are, and how well you can handle it. There are several possibilities that if you have an anger problem, you may have it in mind. When you see yourself acting incorrectly, out of control, signs that are alarming you will have to ask for help because you are not handling anger correctly.

In a process of calm and harmony, you must discover what it is that causes you so much anger.

You cannot give vent to anger as they abuse it and use it as a license to hurt others. Unintentionally, people who go through duels tend to hurt others, but that is caused by a factor of contained anger at what happened, it is not something personal or directed at you. Even if you sink with anger, you must clarify everything so that you can deal with the situation.

Keys to work on

• Prior assessment of the person's health status. Before starting therapy, is recommended that the patient undergo a medical examination to find out her/his health status and the presence or absence of other pathologies.

• It also requires a firm commitment on the part of the person that they are going to follow psychological therapy.

• When working on anger, it is advisable to use cognitive restructuring by identifying limiting and irrational thoughts. It will also facilitate the emotional drain, recreation, and resources to appease that hidden emotional discomfort.

Topic # 8

GUILTY FEELING

First, a duel at this stage can be very strong, who has not felt guilt for something. Guilt is part of making you feel aware that something is wrong or that you did something, in a mechanical way to act on whatever it is. Yes, you can feel guilty for no reason, and it is normal, the key here is that you do not live with guilt or things that you do not have control.

Guilt is a negative emotion that, and I know that no one likes to go through this. But it is essential that it happens to adapt to the new reality that must be lived. Between colleagues and I concluded that guilt is a painful affect that arises according to belief, looking at it as a feeling of having crossed personal or social ethical norms.

In a duel, even if you are not at fault, the guilt will arise from a fault, but it is not, and especially if you have nothing to do with what happened. The function is to raise awareness of what happened, and in a way to help to be able to recover in the life that continues. This is based on moral conscience, which begins in childhood, that is when it develops and is influenced by different people and how they are educated on the subject.

You will know that there are people who tend to confuse the emotion of guilt with shame, adding more to the discomfort that is being experienced. Keep in mind that emotions can feed back into each other, and that is dangerous and more if you do not know how to control emotions. Shame is another topic that is not part of any grief. Yes, you may be ashamed of your behavior while living the emotions, but that is not to be ashamed, it is brave to let out the pain and that energy.

Let's examine guilt:

Simple, to understand the fault you must know the elements:

1. Casual act, real or imagined

2. Negative perception and self-assessment

3. Negative emotion that comes from guilt.

Two types of guilt:

1. Healthy or manifest guilt: it comes because of a real damage that we may cause. It is useful to know that it helps to respect the rules and not disturb others. it is a type of punishment

2. Morbid guilt: there is no fault to justify this feeling. This type of guilt is destructive and will not let you

adapt to the new reality. Be careful, if the fault does not work well, it can occur by excess or by default. It simply does not fulfill the function of adaptation.

Keep an eye on this:

1. Let's accept that we did something wrong, but let's move on.

2. Let's learn from our actions and behaviors.

Topic #9

FEELING OF ANXIETY

What is anxiety?

Anxiety is a feeling of fear, awe, and restlessness. It can cause you to feel sweaty, feel a little restless and often tense, and the palpitations to be something out of the ordinary. And yes, it is something normal that stands out from stress. For example, in a work situation you could have anxiety about a situation that arises, perhaps before a test and even before making an important decision. Believe it or not, anxiety can help you face certain situations, it can also give you a boost of energy and even focus, for people with some type of anxiety disorder, fear is not temporary and can be something that overwhelms you.

What are anxiety disorders?

Anxiety disorders are sympathies in which the anxiety does not go away and can get worse over time. Symptoms can interfere with daily activities, such as performance at work, school, and relationships with those around you.

Types of anxiety disorders:

These are several types of anxiety disorders:

1. Generalized anxiety disorder: people tend to worry about common things like health, money, work, and family. But the level of worry is so excessive and overcomes almost every day, and this lasts at least 6 consecutive months.

2. Panic disorder: this type of people suffer recurrent panic attacks, they are repetitive and very sudden moments of intense fear without being in any danger. These attacks come quickly and can last for long minutes or longer.

3. Phobias: these types of people have an intense fear of something that represents little or no real danger. Example, fear of spiders, of flying, going to crowded places, or being in a social situation (this is known as social anxiety).

What causes anxiety disorders?

The cause of the anxiety has not been known. But there are factors like genetics, biology and brain chemistry, stress, and your environment. Now in a duel, the genetics, biology, and chemistry of the brain are altered by what happened, being the duel a factor of stress and environment that is being lived.

Who is at risk for anxiety disorders?

Risk factors for different types of anxiety disorders can vary. Example, women may experience more generalized anxiety and phobias, but social anxiety affects both equally. As in everything, these are general risk factors for all disorders:

A. Certain personality traits, perhaps being shy, withdrawn.

B. Traumatic events in childhood or adulthood.

C. Family history of anxiety or mental disorders.

D. Physical health, such as torus problems or arrhythmia

Anxiety symptoms:

1. Anxious thoughts or beliefs that are difficult to control. They are restless, tense, and interfere with

daily life. It will not go away, and it will even get worse over time.

2. Physical symptoms, pounding heartbeat, unexplained aches and pains, dizziness, and even shortness of breath.

3. Changes in conduct and behaviors, perhaps avoiding everyday activities that you used to do.

* KEEP IN MIND * using high caffeine content, or other substances can worsen symptoms.

This list is not complete, but we are not going to delve into the subject because it is not about mental disorders but about anxiety in duels.

When you are living a duel, you experience rave or uneasiness of uncertainty about the future to come. These certain things can appear as part of grief anxiety:

1. Difficulty solving problems

2. Nervousness

3. Muscle tension

4. Tremors

5. Nightmares

6. Respiratory problems

7. Feeling of knot in the stomach

8. Feeling of loss of control

Prevent anxiety:

1. Get informed

2. Talk to someone

3. Participate in many more things

4. Spend time with more people

5. Learn relaxation technique

Keep in mind:

1. In the midst of anxiety the person is more demanding

2. You can deprive yourself of sleep

3. Being busy may fail, if in the past it worked

What I can do:

1. Analyze what makes you feel anxious

2. Talk to someone about what worries you or causes you fear

3. Keep in mind that being sad and afraid is okay

4. Don't be afraid to seek therapy, a support group, or whatever you feel comfortable with.

5. Analyze if you experienced similar feelings in the past and how you got out of the hole

6. Try and apply relaxation techniques

7. Test and apply visualization techniques

8. Write down each emotion, mood, and thoughts

9. If necessary, take medications that help with

anxiety

Topic # 10

EMOTIONAL FATIGUE

Emotional fatigue is a type of extreme tiredness, also a generalized weakness that manifests itself physically as well as emotionally. In the physical form, it usually appears as the day progresses, due to so much accumulation of tensions to which we expose our body, on the other hand, the emotional form is more perceptible in the morning.

Honestly speaking, haven't you ever thought, when the alarm sounded, just thinking about everything that I still have ahead of me makes me feel tired? I don't feel like struggling with anything today; I feel that no matter how much I do, nothing turns out the way I want, etc. These types of manifestations are consequences of something called EMOTIONAL FATIGUE.

An emotional exhaustion or depletion that is linked with feelings of anguish, stress, and depression. This happens at an extremely high level that there are attention problems and the feeling that thoughts are slowing down more and more. But will it be possible to fight it? Or what is more imperative, can we avoid it so that it does not come to besiege us? The answer is simple YES. Follow me and let's explore a little more:

The form of prevention will always be to learn to manage ourselves emotionally in a healthy way. How do I do that? Taking our emotions as a guide. These will serve as a compass, while the positive feelings will tell us that we are on the right path, the most annoying feelings will tell us that something we must change to get closer to the balance we want.

Now you ask yourself, why focus on emotions and not thought? I tell you, none is exclusive, but while thinking is something that can deceive us, since we control our thoughts, that is, we control our beliefs, and emotions come abruptly, they are like that. Here's an example, I don't choose who I fall in love with, I just fall in love. And why am I talking about positive or negative emotional sensations and not just positive or negative emotions? Simple, because all emotion is positive, in another hand, it is that they are pleasant or not, but above all the emotions are wanting to say something. As a mandate and respect for ourselves, we must find out.

Incidentally, how do we combat emotional fatigue when it has already become our companion?

A. Acknowledge it. We may think that there is nothing, but there is. Everything is cause and effect: a decision, a thought, a bad move of life, etc. This could trigger it: extreme worry, unresolved issues, mental disorder, daily fights, work problems, toxic relationships, and more.

B. Identified. Once you know where the emotional fatigue comes from then it is time for you to face it, stay here and see how.

C. Calm the mind. It begins with breathing exercises, meditation, filling the mind, etc. These exercises lower the heart rate and with it the feeling of peace and relaxation invades your mind and life, which is something delicious.

D. Sleep. You cannot alter the sleep cycle, that deregulates the mind. Learn to sleep.

E. Water. Water is essential for life; it is gasoline for the mind. You must drink an average of two liters of water a day and rest assured that you will feel serenity every day. Drink water, that will help oxygenate the brain and blood and more when you first wake up. So, on an empty stomach drink water. WATER, no sodas, juice, coffee. Sure? I hope so.

F. Exercises. This will help toxins to leave the body and create endorphins, the famous hormone of HAPPINESS.

G. Priorities. You can't do everything at once, so set a list of achievable goals and go after them.

H. Limits. We own our lives, no one else rules us, only us, are you selfish? NOOOOOOOOO, it is to be well with oneself which is imperative in this.

My books:

Follow me:

IG: DONRAFAEL1946

TWITTER: DRRAFAELSTEWART

FACEBOOK: RAFAEL STEWART

This version is part of the series Duelo en 2 Tiempos, this book was translated from its original version.

This book is part of the series that I started in 2020, I worked hard on these 2 volumes because I am attached to the subject and it's what I know. I am forever grateful for all the people that have read and have attended my seminars and seem my videos to become a better person. I am humbled by the love and respect I have received from everyone throughout this journey.

I hope you enjoyed reading through these lines as much as I enjoyed writing them.

Be grateful with everything you've got and everything you've lost, because those things you lost mean there were no part of you. Be open for better things and life will reward you.

God bless you,

Rafael Stewart

Quito, Ecuador Nov 23, 2021, 1:37 P.M

Thank you!

Thank you, God, for giving another day to breath and be among those that I love. Thank you Mami for always being there and for your love and support, I love you! Thank you to my baby Jonathan for always inspiring me and helping me thorough this journey of writing. You helped me tremendously with this work. Thank you, Kiara, my baby dog for always being there, sitting behind me and being with me all the time, while I write these lines I was sitting in Quito, afraid because we recently had an earthquake, and that feeling was hideous. I miss everyone and everything, but we will be there soon. Thank you to all my family members and those that supported me and accepted me as I am.

With love,

Rafael

P.S. I hope you can heal those emotional wounds!

www.ingramcontent.com/pod-product-compliance
Lightning Source LLC
Chambersburg PA
CBHW061620130726
47996CB00003B/1057